Beyond the Blue

Heaven Waits for You

Roxanne Drury

Scripture taken from THE HOLY BIBLE, NEW INTERNATIONAL VERSION®, NIV® Copyright
© 1973, 1978, 1984, 2011 by Biblica, Inc.® Used by permission. All rights reserved worldwide.

WestBow Press books may be ordered through booksellers or by contacting:

WestBow Press
A Division of Thomas Nelson & Zondervan
1663 Liberty Drive
Bloomington, IN 47403
www.westbowpress.com
1 (866) 928-1240

Because of the dynamic nature of the Internet, any web addresses or links contained
in this book may have changed since publication and may no longer be valid. The views
expressed in this work are solely those of the author and do not necessarily reflect the views
of the publisher, and the publisher hereby disclaims any responsibility for them.

Any people depicted in stock imagery provided by Getty Images are models,
and such images are being used for illustrative purposes only.
Certain stock imagery © Getty Images.

ISBN: 978-1-9736-5036-2 (sc)
ISBN: 978-1-9736-5037-9 (e)

Library of Congress Control Number: 2019900104

Print information available on the last page.

WestBow Press rev. date: 10/18/2019

WESTBOW
PRESS®
A DIVISION OF THOMAS NELSON
& ZONDERVAN

Dedication: For my heavenly Father who has made room for me in His heavenly home. Thank You for Your divine guidance through this process and Your inspiration all those years ago.

Acknowledgment:

Thanks to my support and encouragement network of family and friends: Darrell & Janet McClure, Betty Yeider and most importantly, my wonderful husband, Steve, who has always been there cheering me on with enthusiasm or providing a voice of reason and being exactly what I needed when I needed it always with love and kindness.

Scripture Gem: "Do not let your hearts be troubled. Trust in God; also trust in me. In my Father's house are many rooms; if it were not so, I would have told you. I am going there to prepare a place for you." John 14:1, 2 NIV

Other NIV scripture references: Revelation 21: 1-27, Revelation 3: 4-5, 4:3, 5:11, 7:15, 22: 1-5,14, 19:9, 20:15, 22:1-5, 14, Isaiah 11: 6-9, Isaiah 25: 6-8, Isaiah 65: 17-25, Phillipians3:21, John 14:1,2,6, Genesis 1:24-25, John 3:16, Romans 3:23, I Corinthians 15: 3,4, John 1:12 NIV

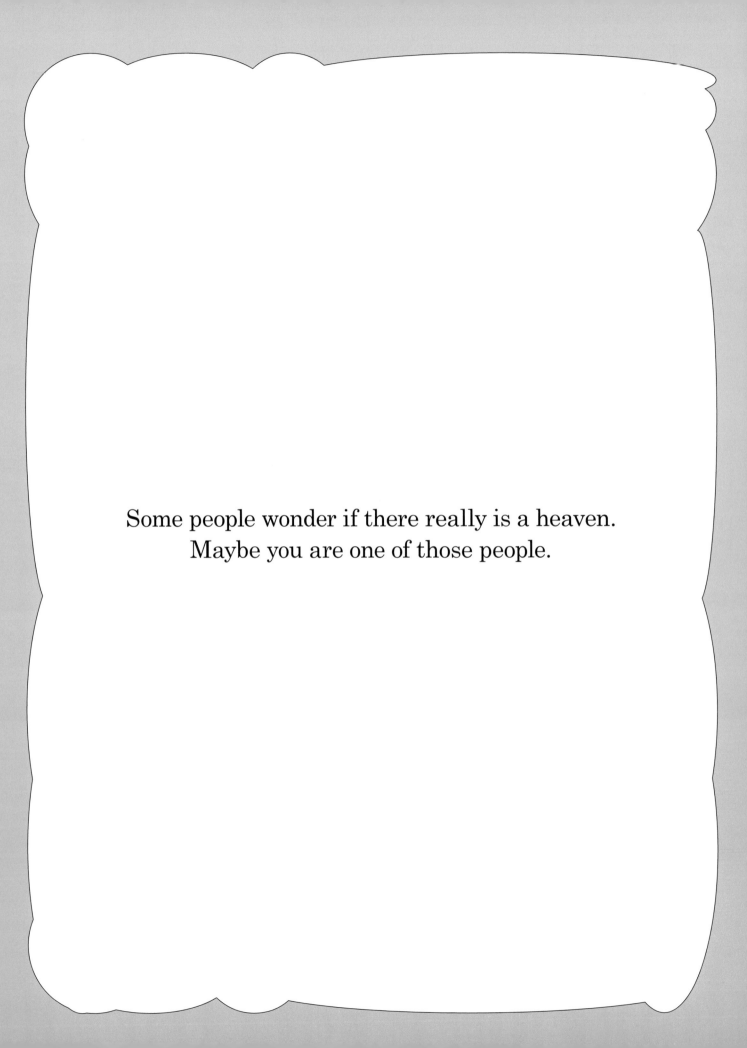

Some people wonder if there really is a heaven.
Maybe you are one of those people.

Well, the Bible says…

Beyond the great beyond there is a beautiful place called heaven. It is more beautiful than anything you can ever imagine. Heaven is beautiful because God lives there. All of God's angels live there too. There is no night in heaven because God's light shines so very bright and beautiful. Only truth and beauty exist in heaven and that makes it perfect!

All the people that love God and know Jesus
go to live in heaven when this life is over. That
makes heaven a very, very special place.

God promised that there would be a place ready in
heaven for everyone that believes in Him and knows His
Son, Jesus. Jesus called heaven "His Father's house".
God's plan was for Jesus to go to heaven and get things
ready and that's just what He did. There are many,
many rooms there – rooms enough for everyone.

Some people wonder what it will be like in heaven. Perhaps you are one of those people. You might wonder if people will get hungry in heaven or what they wear or maybe even if there will be toys or swimming pools.

The Bible tells us that God will make a wonderfully delicious supper for everyone that lives in heaven. There will be lots of good food to eat and good drinks to drink. Our bodies will be different in heaven, though, they will be perfect, and so I imagine we can eat if we want to but we won't need food as we do now.

In heaven, we will be dressed in sparkling white clothes. They will stay clean all the time. Imagine that!! The Bible says that heaven is a happy place. That makes me think that we will have more fun being in heaven than playing with toys or going swimming.

The Bible also says God's people will serve Him, so even the work God has for us to do will make us happy. Because God loves us so much, I am sure of one thing – He will give us everything we need.

You might wonder if your dog or cat or pet fish will be in heaven. The Bible doesn't really answer that question exactly, so we are not sure where our pets go when their life is over. But we do know there are animals in heaven like wolves and lambs, leopards and goats, calves and lions and cows and bears. Our animal pets are different than people but they were still created by God and He said they were good. We can trust God to do what is good for all of His creations including our pets.

In heaven -
There are no tears -
      There is no pain -
           and there is no sickness.
No one is ever sad or scared and no one ever gets hurt.
That means heaven is filled with joy and love and laughter.

Heaven is a safe place, too. There are high walls and gates to protect everyone that lives in heaven. The gates will never be shut and nothing and no one bad will ever enter the city. There are three gates on the east, three gates on the north, three gates on the south, and three gates on the west of the city. Each gate is made of one shiny pearl and near each gate is an angel. WOW! That will be amazing to see!

All of heaven is bright and shines like a brilliant jewel. In fact, the Bible says the streets and the cities in heaven are made of pure gold. Gold is definitely bright and shiny! The high walls of the city have twelve foundations and each foundation is covered with a different kind of jewel. So the foundations of the walls probably look like an exquisite shiny rainbow.

The Bible says there is a river that flows through the city and it is bright and clear as crystal. On either side of the river, the tree of life grows. It is an unusual kind of tree with twelve kinds of fruit. The tree produces fruit all the time and everyone in heaven will be able to eat from the tree of life whenever they want to.

Heaven is a place that God set apart for all those that love Him and His Son, Jesus. He wanted us to have a place where we could live with Him forever.

So, when you look up in the sky and see the beautiful bright sun shining through the clouds –

                              think of heaven, and remember -

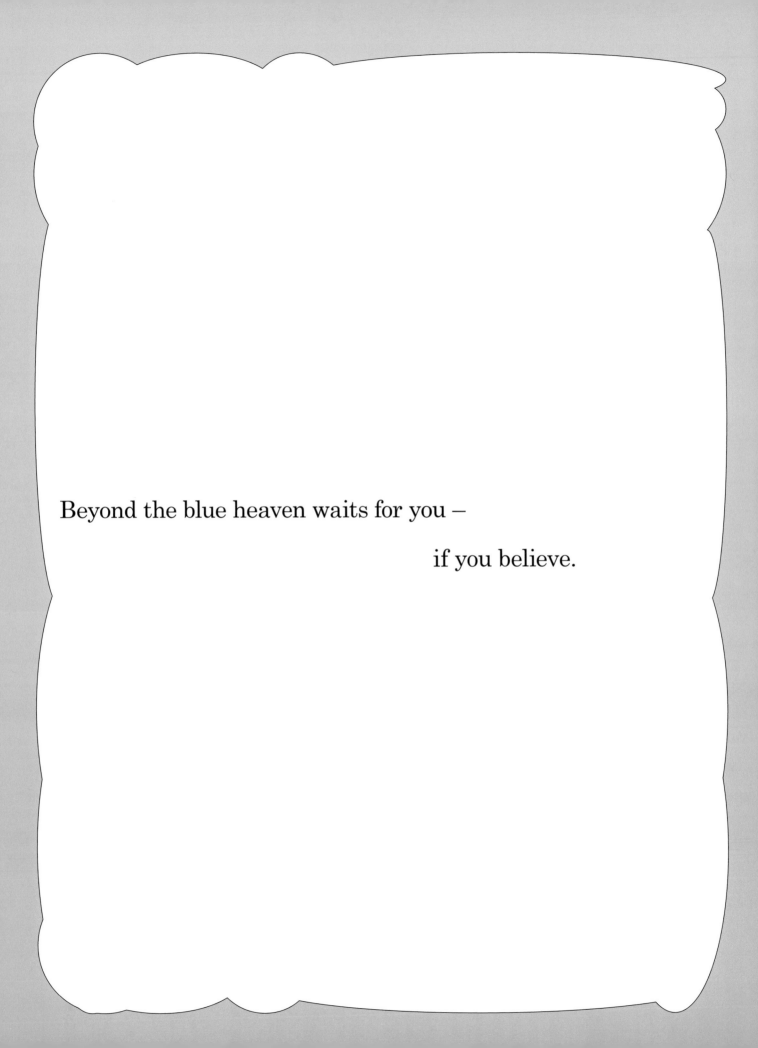

Beyond the blue heaven waits for you –

                              if you believe.

Dear Parents:

If you are reading this book for the first time and have never made a commitment to Jesus as your Savior, I hope you won't wait one more minute to do so. Just follow the ABC steps outlined on the next page and then share what you have done and this book with your child. God's love and saving grace was meant to be shared.

I hope you will find this little book helpful in opening up a conversation with your child about their eternal life. We, as parents have an awesome responsibility in the rearing of our children. The fact that we must care for their material needs is obvious. Where we sometimes flounder is in tending to their spiritual needs. We leave it to the church or feel inadequate. Guess what, mom or dad, God can work through you! He wants to work through you in the life of your child. He doesn't need us to be eloquent speakers, or have all the answers; He just needs us to open up the conversation. The Holy Spirit will do the rest through you and in your child.

Here are some simple steps to take that will help you:

1. Pray before reading this book with your child. Ask God to help you ask the right questions at the right time and to have the answers to the questions your child might ask.
2. Find a quiet place for you and your child to read this book together. Cuddle up and get cozy.
3. Allow your child time to look at the pictures and ask questions. Answer his or her questions as best you can.
4. If you are sensing that your child might want to make a commitment to Jesus, go ahead and follow the ABC steps outlined on the next page and then ask the question.
5. If your child does not express interest, that's okay, don't force it – everything happens in God's timing. If your child does make a commitment you will want to make sure to keep helping him or her get to know God better by:
   a. Reading the Bible with them or to them every day
   b. Regularly going to church and/or Sunday School
   c. Praying with your child
   d. Reminding them to ask forgiveness when they do things that are wrong

God bless you as you take this heavenly journey, Beyond the Blue!

Your friend,
Miss Roxanne

Leading your child to Christ:

Say: God loves you very much and wants to be your forever friend. The wrong choices we make keep us away from God. The Bible calls these wrong choices sin. Everyone makes wrong choices sometimes and everyone needs to ask for God's forgiveness. God wants to and will forgive you because He loves you and wants you to live with Him in heaven someday. ["For all have sinned and fall short of the glory of God". Romans 3:23]

Here's what to do:

Admit you sometimes do things that do not please God. (make Him sad)

Say: This is called sin. The Bible says everyone sins and that sin must be punished. The punishment for sin is separation from God.

Ask: Can you think of something you have done that might have made God sad? (disobeying, lying, etc.) The good news is that God had a wonderful plan so we don't have to be separated from Him. He sent His son Jesus. ["For God so loved the world He sent His one and only Son that whoever believes in Him will not die but have eternal life". John 3:16]

Believe in Jesus and what He did for you.

Say: God sent Jesus, His Son, to die on the cross and take our punishment so that we wouldn't have to be separated from God. God did that because He loved you so much. The good news is that Jesus didn't stay dead. He came back to life and now He is in heaven.

Ask: Do you believe that Jesus is God's Son and that He died on the cross to take your punishment so you wouldn't have to be separated from God? ["Christ died for our sins according to the scriptures, that He was buried, that He was raised on the third day according to the scriptures". I Cor 15: 3,4]

Confess (tell) God what you have done wrong and ask Him to forgive you.

Say: You can tell God that you believe in His Son, Jesus and want Jesus to come into your life and be with you always as your forever friend. You can claim Jesus as your Savior and become a child of God. ["Yet to all who received Him, to those who believed in His name, He gave the right to become children of God". John 1:12]

Ask: Do you think you would like to talk to God about that now?

Help your child pray this prayer:

Dear God:

Thank You for loving me so much that You sent Your Son, Jesus, to die on the cross to take my punishment. I believe He died for me and then came back to life. Please forgive me for the things I have done that made You sad. I want Jesus to come into my life and be my forever friend. Please help me do things Your way from now on. In Jesus' Name. Amen

If you or your child accepted Jesus as Savior as a result of reading this book, we would love to hear about it so we can pray for you and your child.
Please e-mail us at **glorylandbooks@gmail.com**

Please visit me at: www.roxannedrury.com

Printed in the United States
By Bookmasters